THE MONASTERY
OF AGIOS NEOPHYTOS

History and Art
(A Short Guide)

© Holy Royal and Stavropegiac Monastery of Saint Neophytos

ISBN: 9963-614-03-5

First edition 1998

Second edition 2005

THE MONASTERY OF AGIOS NEOPHYTOS

History and Art

(A Short Guide)

A. PAPAGEORGIOU

Former Director of the Department of Antiquities

NICOSIA, CYPRUS

2005

PAFOS AREA

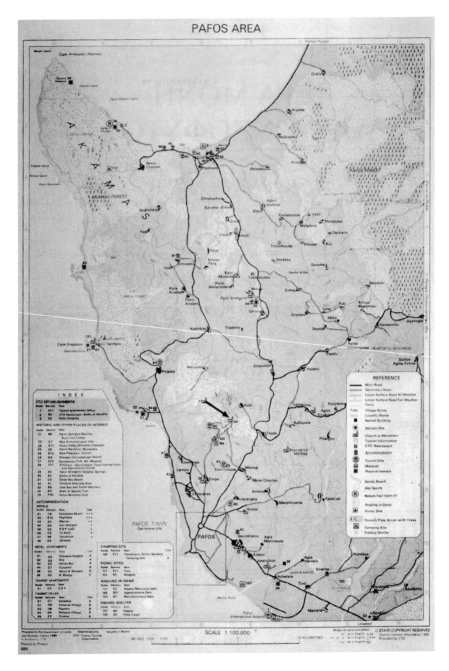

A map of the area of Paphos.

AGIOS NEOPHYTOS MONASTERY

The location of the Monastery

The Agios Neophytos Monastery is built at the extreme end of a deep valley about ten kilometres northwest of the town of Paphos, at 412m above sea level. The view from the monastery of the town and the sea is fantastic. Two roads lead from the town of Paphos to the Monastery. The one through the villages of Emba and Tala and the other through the villages of Mesogi and Tremithousa. The two roads link up at some distance from the Monastery. The visitor in approaching the Monastery sees in front of him the monastery buildings in a Π shape which surround the Catholikon (the main church) of the Monastery from the west, the south and the east. The church is built on the north side of the atrium. The Monastery is surrounded on the north, the east and the west by high hills. Particularly steep is the hill which is to the west and at a distance of about one hundred metres from the Monastery. Between the Monastery and this hill there is today a square. To the west of this square there is a torrent. A narrow bridge built in 1877 joins the square to the nearby hill on the east side of which there is the hewn Engleistra of St. Neophytos. Opposite the Engleistra and to the east of the Monastery there is Melissovounos, in a natural cave of which there were, according to tradition, wild bees which gave the hill its name. At Melissovounos there are also quarries from which the stones with which the main church and the cells of the Monastery were built were extracted.

1. General view of the Monastery of Agios Neophytos (from the air).

SAINT NEOPHYTOS AND THE ENGLEISTRA

The founder of the Monastery Saint Neophytos was born in 1134 at the township of Lefkara, as he himself says in his Ritual Ordinance. He was born into a poor, rural, large family. Since childhood he was drawn to the teachings of Christ and monastic life. For this reason when his parents arranged for him to be engaged to be married at the age of 18 (at that time marriage affairs were handled by the parents without those to be married being consulted) Saint Neophytos left his native village and went secretly to the Agios Ioannis Chrysostomos Monastery at Koutsovendi to live as an ascetic. As the Saint was illiterate the abbot of the Monastery Maximos entrusted to him the task of cultivating the vineyards of the Monastery at "Stoupais" locality. For five years Neophytos's task was tending the vineyards. Having a strong desire to learn and being endowed with a strong will he acquired during this period some basic education and learned the Psalter by heart. Then the abbot called him back to the Monastery and asked him to carry out duties of assistant sacristan, a post in which he served for two years.

But the five–year stay at Stoupais reinforced his inborn inclination for the ascetic life. Thus he asked the then abbot of the Monastery to allow him to become a hermit. But the abbot, due to the young age of the Saint, did not allow him to leave the Monastery and live as a hermit in one of the caves which were, a little higher, in the area of the Monastery. The Saint then asked for permission to go to Jerusalem on a pilgrimage to the Holy Land which was consecrated by Christ through His life, His crucifixion and His resurrection. He hoped that by going to the Holy Land he would find some hermit to lead him to the ascetic life. He tried, by wandering for six months in the Holy Land, which was at the time under the occupation of the Arabs and the Crusaders, to achieve his aim but without success. Thus he returned to Cyprus and went back to Agios Chrysostomos Monastery at Koutsovendi. He tried again to persuade the abbot to allow him to lead an ascetic life but to no avail. The refusal of the abbot to respond to his fervent desire to live an ascetic life caused the Saint to leave Agios

2. The inscription of 1503 and Saints Antonios, Arsenios and Euthymios.

Chrysostomos Monastery and to go to Latros mountain in Asia Minor which was a major monastic community and to which another Cypriot, the Patriarch of Constantinople, Gregorios II the Cypriot (1283–1289) sought refuge in 1289. He went to Paphos in the hope of finding a ship that would carry him there. But at the port of Paphos he was arrested as a fugitive and imprisoned while those guarding him stole from him two coins with which he was to pay the fare. When as a result of the mediation of pious men he was released from prison the following day, as he himself says, not having the fare any longer, he was forced to look for a hermitage inland. Thus he reached the cliff and the small natural cave which he transformed into his Engleistra. This happened in 1159. For three months (24 June, Day of the Birth of St. John the Baptist, until September) he explored the area to determine whether it was deserted and quiet. He then started hewing the small natural cave, removing the rotten rocks and enlarging it for a whole year until the feast of the Exultation of the True Cross 14 September 1160. In this way he created the church of the Engleistra and one cell in which he dug his grave. Five years later he looked for and found a piece of the True Cross which he put in a cross-shaped niche of a wooden cross which survives until today. But the piece of the True Cross has been lost. Originally the wooden cross was placed in a cross–shaped niche on the east wall of the Engleistra. The wall had been built by the Saint himself in order to close the cave. At that time, as Saint Neophytos informs us, the episcopal throne of Paphos was vacant. But in the seventh year of the stay of the Saint in the Engleistra Vasilios Kinnamos was ordained bishop of Paphos. The Bishop of Paphos was favourably disposed towards Saint Neophytos and for four years pressed him to agree to be ordained priest. In 1170 the Bishop of Paphos Kinnamos ordained the Saint priest and persuaded him to take a pupil after providing him with the necessary food ration. From that time the Engleistra started to be enlarged and embellished and all along the cliff cells were hewn. Even though the Saint originally wanted a limited number of monks, later, in his second Ritual Ordinance which he wrote in 1214, he fixes their number at 15 or 18.

The reputation of the Saint started to spread everywhere and soon the number of the visitors to the Engleistra increased considerably. The visitors, as was to be expected, interfered with the solitude of the Saint who in order to avoid this interference dug in 1197 high above the Engleistra another cell, the "New Zion" as he called it, to which he sought refuge from the visitors. But in order to be able to attend church services and to participate in the Eucharist he dug above the church of the Engleistra a small cell, the "Hagiastirion", which he joined through a rectangular hole to the church. More to the north of "New Sion" and at a higher level he dug another cell, that of St. John the Baptist.

In the meantime, dramatic events had taken place in Cyprus which had cut it off from Byzantium and brought misery to the Church and its people. In 1184 Isaakios Komnenos declared himself ruler of Cyprus and his seven–year tyranny brought much misery to Cyprus. In 1191 Cyprus was occupied by Richard the Lionheart King of England, who, after looting it, sold it to the Templars and the next year, following a rising that was suppressed in bloodshed by the rulers, he sold it to the deposed king of Jerusalem, Guy de Lusignan, who established the Frankish Kingdom in Cyprus. Land owners were deprived of their property and the Greek inhabitants of Cyprus were turned into serfs. The sad situation that prevailed in Cyprus is described very vividly by the Saint in a short letter which is known under the title "About the misfortunes of Cyprus" and which he wrote in 1196.

Poverty and misery caused many people to seek food at the Monasteries one of which was the Engleistra. The Saint very reluctantly responded to the entreaties of the monks and allowed the acquisition of land and vineyards and a few animals so that food could be provided to all those who went to the Engleistra.

The date of the death of St. Neophytos is not known. In 1214 he dictated his Ritual Ordinance to the Secretary of the Paphos Bishopric, Vasilios. The manuscript, which has survived until today at the university library of Edinburgh, has corrections made by the Saint himself. Consequently, he must have died after 1214 after previously appointing as his successor his nephew Isaias who was "oekonomos"

(= the monk responsible for the supplies of the Engleistra and the distribution of the food) of the Engleistra. It is generally accepted that the Saint was buried according to his instructions in the grave he himself had prepared, in a wooden coffin made of pine, cedar and cypress wood he had made before his death. His successor, Isaias, following the instructions of the Saint, closed with a wall the opening created to place the coffin in the grave and decorated the wall with paintings so that it may not be visible. This resulted in the exact place of the burial of the Saint being forgotten with the passage of time and the Russian monk Vasili Barsky said in 1745 that the Eucharist was celebrated on the grave of the Saint.

Saint Neophytos was a very prolific writer. Despite the fact that he learned to read and write after the age of 18 he is perhaps the most prolific Middle byzantine writer. Apart from his sermons, he wrote commentaries on the Bible and other works which contain valuable information about the lives of the saints and the history of Cyprus. The Agios Neophytos Monastery has recently published the works of the Saint in four volumes.

The Engleistra in 1214

Saint Neophytos gives us a detailed description of the Engleistra in his second Ritual Ordinance which was written 55 years after he settled in the Engleistra, that is in 1214 (1159+55).

The description is contained in the 20th chapter of his Ordinance: "A little beyond the Engleistra we built a gate... and then a bakery, a kitchen, a store for storing crops, various cells and another two in the garden; also the cells near the fountain which were used, those downstairs as stables and barn and those upstairs as living quarters; then the larder and the five–arched verandah above it and within it the refectory hewn within these arches; then the narthex and the sacristy over it and above the latter the Agiastirion in which I participate in the eucharist and hear the holy hymns and above the said Agiastirion the more recent Engleistra New Sion. The whole work is a work of God's Providence. And another cell, called the cell of St. John the Baptist, hewn in the cliff, and also the Major Structure in the torrent with many arches more diligently built".

Very few of the buildings the Saint mentions have survived. Today there are the church and the bema and the cell of the Saint where his grave is also situated, the narthex with the sacristy and the "Agiastirion" and the Refectory of the Monastery. The five–arched verandah which most probably survived until 1735 when Vasili Barsky visited the Monastery and diligently made a drawing, disappeared later and was replaced by a wooden structure which was already destroyed at the end of the 19th century.In 1963 in order to prop up the rock in which the Engleistra is hewn a new five–arched verandah was constructed which includes the Engleistra, the Narthex with the sacristy which is above it and the Refectory. The "Agiastirion" and a large part of "New Sion" and of the cell of St. John the Baptist still survive.

The Engleistra, that is the church of the True Cross and the cell of Saint Neophytos, were decorated with wall paintings in 1183, as he himself says in his Rules of the Monastery. This decoration is evidenced also by the half-destroyed inscription in the cell of the Saint. However, the main church, not the bema, was decorated, for a reason not known, again with wall paintings which have survived until today. This second decoration was presumably done after 1214, since the Saint in his Ritual Ordinance mentions only one decoration of the Engleistra, that of 1183.

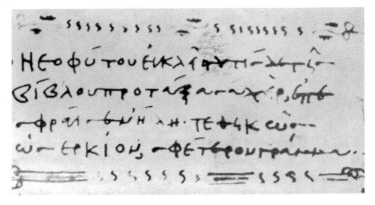

Manuscript of Saint Neophytos

12

HISTORY OF THE MONASTERY

It is taken for granted that Saint Neophytos was succeeded as abbot of the Engleistra by Isaias whom he himself had appointed as his successor. Nothing is known about Isaias. The present decoration of the Engleistra, which replaced that of 1183, was probably done at the time of Isaias. No abbot of the Agios Neophytos Monastery other than Isaias is known from the 13th, the 14th and the 15th centuries. Abbot Sofronios, whose signature has survived on f.216 of the manuscript Paris. Gr. 1492 which belonged to the Engleistra, most probably lived at the end of the 15th century. In any case the Monastery continued to exist and to thrive. In the 15th century the Monastery of Agios Epiphanios of Kouvouklion (Kouklia) is referred to as annexe of the Agios Neophytos Monastery. This monastery is as old as the Engleistra and there is reference to it in 1204. The Monastery of Agios Epiphanios owned during this time property and the churches of Agios Demetrios at Nicocleia and of Agios Andronikos and Athanasia at Mandria (in Paphos).

In 1503, a monk named Neophytos met the expenses for the "renovation" of some of the wall paintings in the church of the Engleistra (Hospitality of Abraham, the Last Supper, the Washing of the Feet, and small sections of the Prayer in the garden of Gethsemane, the Betrayal and the Ascension) and the Pantocrator, the Virgin and St. John the Baptist in the west part of the ceiling of the bema). Apparently the same Neophytos met the expenses for the icons of Saint Neophytos and the Dormition of the Virgin which are today in the Museum of the Monastery. Is he the same person as the monk Neophytos who died in 1512 and is described as the "new founder" of the Engleistra in a note in the codex Paris. Graecus 1461? If he is the same monk then he must no doubt have spent a lot of money on the renovation of the Monastery. The main church of the Monastery and the first cells round it were probably constructed with money provided by this Neophytos. Only then would his description as "new founder" be justified. Indeed the typological and morphological characteristics of the church indicate that it was built early in the 16th century.

Strangely though the new large church of the Monastery of the Engleistra was not built at the site suggested by Saint Neophytos in his Ordinance "at the back of these apses (of the Great Construction with many apses in the Torrent) may God grant that another church may be built dedicated to the Trinity". Nor was it dedicated to the Trinity. The new church was dedicated to the Virgin and was built 100 metres east of the Engleistra, perhaps because the site indicated by the Saint was judged to be unsuitable on account of the torrent and the limited space.

In the same codex (Paris Gr. 1461) the death on 11 April of the Abbot of the Engleistra, Ioakeim, is noted. This Ioakeim is apparently other than the former abbot Ioakeim, who is depicted kneeling in the icon of Panagia Engleistriani, which dates back to the first half of the 16th century.

Another Abbot of the first half of the 16th century is Timotheos. His name was mentioned in the dedicatory inscription of the icon of the Dormition of the Virgin which is today in the Museum of the Monastery. This inscription is today half destroyed.

In 1523 the Patriarch of Constantinople Ieremias I visited the Engleistra of Saint Neophytos and remained in it seventeen days. The visit of Patriarch Ieremias is mentioned in codexes Coisl. 65, Coisl. 105 and Paris Gr. 1627 of the National Library of Paris which originally belonged to the Agios Neophytos Monstery.

In 1570 Cyprus was conquered by the Turks who looted it systematically. The monasteries too were looted including the Agios Neophytos Monastery. In 1585 on instructions from Sultan Murat the monasteries, and particularly the Agios Neophytos Monastery, were sold and the monks were forced to scatter. At that time a certain Yerasimos was the abbot. The Monastery was most probably abandoned at the time while the main church, which had perhaps been damaged by the earthquake of 1577, lost a large part of its wall paintings. At that time the abbot of the Monastery was a certain Gerasimos.

The renaissance of the Monastery was achieved by monk Leontios. Leontios gathered monks and he himself was ordained abbot. In 1611 he asked Archbishop Christodoulos to declare the Monastery a stavropegiac, which the Archbishop did with the unanimous agreement of the Bishop of Paphos Leontios. In order to safeguard the independence of the Monastery from the Bishops of Paphos, Abbot Leontios asked in 1631 the Patriarch of Constantinople Kyrillos Loukaris to confirm the stavropegiac of the Monastery. Kyrillos Loukaris who had a few yars earlier visited Cyprus, when he was still Patriarch of Alexandria, issued a Patriarchal Ordinance with which he declared the Agios Neophytos Monastery stavropegiac. The Ordinance was signed by the members of the Synod of the Patriarchate and the Archbishop of Cyprus Christodoulos. The Ordinance was later signed also by the Archbishops of Cyprus Nikiforos, Iacovos I, Germanos, Iacovos II, Silvestros and Philotheos and the Bishops of Paphos Makarios and Germanos. The independence of the Monastery from the Bishop of Paphos and the efforts of the active abbot Leontios restored the Monastery almost to its old glamour and fame. The date of the death of abbot Leontios is not known. It seems, however, that the Monastery, also on account of Turkish greed, started to decline again. It is not known who succeeded Leontios as abbot. The next known abbot was Nikiforos who died in 1724. He was succeeded by Ioannikios who died before 1735 and he was succeeded by Timotheos. In the summer of 1735 the Russian monk Vasili Barsky visited the Agios Neophytos Monastery. As he says in his "Wanderings" he found only two or three monks at the Monastery which had at the time ten cells. Most of the cells were empty. According to Barsky, the founder of the Monastery was forgotten, not of course Saint Neophytos about whom the monks knew that he had lived in the Engleistra where there was his grave covered with a marble slab on which the Eucharist was celebrated. But the grave, as he heard, was in the bema and had not yet been uncovered. Thus the location of the grave of Saint Neophytos had been completely forgotten. Barsky describes the main church of the

Monastery which he compares to the church of Agios Mamas at Morphou which is indeed of the same architectural type. Barsky made most detailed drawings of the Monastery and the Engleistra of Saint Neophytos. The abbot of the Monastery Timotheos was hospitable and soft spoken as Barsky says. In 1746 Athanasios became the new abbot and made efforts to protect and increase the property of the Monastery. At the time Athanasios was Abbot the grave and the relics of Saint Neophytos were found, most probably, in 1756. The relics were transferred to the main church of the Monastery.

In 1779 Abbot Ioannikios repaired the "church of Agia Engleistra". But what is probably meant by church of Agia Engleistra was the replacement of the five-arched veranda, which had been destroyed, with wooden construction which deteriorated by the late 19th century. In the same year he spent money for the publication of the Ritual Ordinance, of the Book of the Divine Sign and other works and mainly the sermons on the six days of the creation. The publication was supervised by the Archimandrite of the Archbishop Kyprianos in Venice. The successor to Ioannikios Theophanis saw to it that two thrones on either side of the Abbot's throne and pews in the main church of the Monastery, the iconostasis of the church of the Engleistra and the door leading from the narthex to the church of the Engleistra were constructed. Theophanis excelled also as a scribe. He died in 1800 or 1801 and was succeeded in 1801 by Ioakeim Melissovoukas who suffered a horrible death in the hands of the Turks in 1821. Ioakeim in 1818 built the rooms of the east wing of the Monastery. His successors Chrysanthos Mesaritis (1823–1833), Chrysanthos Galatariotis Empirical Doctor (1833–1855), Gregorios (1855–1893), Iacovos Myriantheas (1898–1933) increased the property of the Monastery.

Iacovos was succeded by his nephew Archimandrite Lavrentios (1933–1962) and he for a short time by Archimandrite Leontios (1962) and Sofronios. In 1963 Archimandrite Alexios became abbot. He died in 1972 and was succeeded by Archimandrite Chrysostomos, who in 1978 was elected bishop of Paphos. He was succeeded by the present abbot Leontios who has very actively promoted the publication of the works of Saint Neophytos.

3. General view of the Engleistra of Saint Neophytos.

DESCRIPTION OF THE ENGLEISTRA AND THE AGIOS NEOPHYTOS MONASTERY

THE ENGLEISTRA

The Engleistra of Saint Neophytos is hewn in the steep side of a hill and consists, as we have seen, of the church of the True Cross and its narthex, the cell of the Saint and the Refectory. The cells which were hewn north and south of the Engleistra have been destroyed and only remnants of one cell south of the Engleistra and another two north–east of the Refectory have survived until today.

1. The Narthex

The Engleistra is beyond the torrent. A narrow bridge which was built in 1877 brings the visitor to a narrow stone-built staircase with 23 steps which leads to the narthex of the Engleistra, at a height of 4,75m. The narthex, trapezoidal in shape, is covered with a vault. Two narrow doors, the one on the north wall and the other on the south wall, lead the first to the verandah where the Refectory is and the second to a cell south of the narthex. Above the narthex there is the sacristy which communicates through a small opening with the church. Early in the 16th century the narthex was decorated with wall paintings similar in style to the wall paintings of the main church of the Monastery. Only a few wall paintings have survived. In the spandrel above the entrance to the Engleistra, the Annunciation of the Virgin has survived in good condition. To the right and the left of the entrance wall paintings have survived, badly damaged though. To the left Saint Peter and Saint Gregory the Theologian and on the east side of the nearby niche Saint Gregory Bishop of Nyssa have survived. To the right Saint Paul and Saint Savvas and on the north wall Saint Nicholas have survived but badly damaged.

2. The church

According to the Ritual Ordinance, the church was decorated with wall paintings together with the bema and the cell of the Saint in 1183. But the original decoration of the church has been replaced. The wall paintings which decorate it today were made later, most probably after 1214. Some were made in 1503. In the southwest corner of the church an inscription informs us that the church of the Engleistra was hewn, built and painted with the contribution and much toil of Saint Neophytos in 1196, while in 1503 "the present part of the decoration and many other decorations and essential things were renovated" with money provided by the humble monk Neophytos. The inscription gives wrongly 1196 as the date of the hewing of the Engleistra instead of the correct date 1159 (hewing) and 1183 (decoration) which the Saint himself mentions and is confirmed by the inscription which has survived in the Saint's cell.

The wall paintings which were renovated in 1503 are the Hospitality of Abraham on the south wall, the two first scenes from the Passion Cycle, i.e. the Last Supper and the Washing of the Feet, the lower right corner of the Prayer in the Garden of Gethsemane, a small part of the Betrayal and the Apostles, now very badly damaged, in the scene of the Ascension which is painted at the highest point of the ceiling. Painted on the ceiling are also Moses, David, Isaiah and Jeremiah.

The scenes from the Passion start from the southwest end in the upper part of the walls of the church and continue all along the west and south side. These scenes are the Last Supper, the Washing of the Feet, the Prayer in the Garden of Gethsemane, the Betrayal, Jesus before Pilate, the Road to Calvary, the Crucifixion, the Descent from the Cross, the Lamentation, almost completely destroyed, the Resurrection and the "Don't Touch me" scene.

The lower zone of the west side is decorated with twelve saintly monks who constitute models of monastic life. The inscriptions which are written on the rolls they are holding urge monks to be humble, to repent of their sins and to put their faith in God above love for their parents. These saintly monks are, from the left to the right, Antonios, Arsenios, Efthymios, Amoun Nitriotis, Andronicos, Daniel Skitiotis,

4. Christ before Pilate. Wallpainting of the nave of the Engleistra of Agios Neophytos. After 1214.

5. The road to the Calvary. Wallpainting of the nave of the Engleistra of Saint Neophytos. After 1214.

6. The Crucifixion. Wallpainting of the nave of the Engleistra of Agios Neophytos. After 1214.

Theodosios the Coenobiarch, John of Klimakos, Onoufrios, Makarios, Paisios and Stephanos the Young. With the exception of Stephanos the Young, who lived in the 8th century and suffered martyrdom from the iconoclasts, the other Saintly monks lived in the period of the 4th–6th century. Today the iconostasis occupies two thirds of the north wall. Originally, however, before 1214, there was no iconostasis but a narrow entrance like that which joins the bema to the cell of Saint Neophytos. Indeed above the iconostasis and beneath the decorative band with the vermiculation which is part of the painting of the Passion scenes a combination of the letters O and A, which stand for the words O Agios (the saint), in an earlier layer of painting, has survived. It seems that where there is today the icon of the Virgin on the iconosta-

e Resurrection (Descent into Hell). Wallpainting of the nave of the Engleistra of Agios Neophytos. After 1214.

23

sis of 1796 there was a wall painting of a standing Saint painted on the south side of the wall that separated the main church from the bema. There was another wall painting where on the iconostasis there is the icon of Christ. To the right on the north wall Christ is painted enthroned. On the east end of the wall a small part of a Saintly Bishop has survived.

On the east wall, which at this point forms a rectangular niche, Saint Gregory the Theologian is painted and to the south there is on the wall a cross-shaped niche which originally was larger and had the dimensions of the wooden cross which is today in front of it. This wooden cross, which originally contained a piece of the True Cross which Saint Neophytos had sought and found was in the niche of the wall. Above the horizontal arm of the niche Archangels Michael and Gabriel are painted. On the south side of the niche of the east wall a Saintly Bishop of whom only the upper part of the body has survived is painted.

North of the entrance of the church, on the east wall, a large part of the wall painting depicting Saints Constantine and Helen holding the Cross of Christ which Saint Helen had found has survived, while to the south a very small part of a Saintly Bishop has survived. The wall painting which was directly south of the entrance has not survived. More to the south the head of a donor has survived accompanied by the end of an inscription "[– – – – – – –] humble monk" and in the south end of the east wall the busts of two Saints Stylites, Saint Daniel the Stylite and Saint Symeon, have survived.

But who is the monk donor? As has been pointed out, the wall paintings of the church, with the exception of those made in 1503, must have been made after 1197 when the hole that joined the Agiastirion, from which the Saint attended the church services, with the church, was opened. This is evidenced by the fact that the wall painting of the Ascension was not affected by the opening of this hole. On the other hand, Saint Neophytos in 1214 mentions only one decoration of the Engleistra, that made in 1183. We have seen, however, that of this decoration only a small part has survived beneath the present layer of the wall paintings of the church. Consequently, the wall paintings of the church must have been made after 1214 and most probably by the successor to Saint Neophytos his nephew Isaias. Thus this portrait seems to be depicting Isaias. This accounts for the differences observed between this portrait and the two portraits of Saint Neophytos which are in the bema and in his cell.

3. The wall paintings of the bema

The bema of the church of the True Cross of the Engleistra is on the north side of the church on account of the morphology of the cave which the Saint transformed into a church. The Altar, however is on the east side of the bema. The ceiling of the bema is very uneven. On the west part it is very low. It then ascends steeply and forms an uneven oval "dome" at its highest point over the Altar. In this place the Ascension of Christ is again painted. On the east end the Virgin is painted standing in a frontal position with the hands raised at the sides, as she would be painted in the semidome of a normal apse. The absence of a normal apse resulted in the Virgin being placed between the officiating prelates John Chrysostom, St. Basil, Epiphanios and Nicolaos. On the steep side of the rock opposite the east wall St. Neophytos is painted praying between Archangels Michael and Gabriel. A humble monk himself, wearing the Angel's habit, requests the two Archangels to help him prove worthy and to accompany him in the final resurrection of the dead before the throne of God.

On the low ceiling of the west part of the bema which is almost flat Christ Pantocrator is painted. Round the Pantocrator this poem is written: "O Thou who bearest and holdest everything together in Thy hand, who has stretched out the heavens like a curtain and has founded on the void the earth that nourishes everyone; Thou who has deigned to be born in a cavern, do Thou guard, O saviour, this craggy hill too, by the intercession of the all–pure Mother of God and of the Baptist, both Prophet and forerunner and of the holy hermit Neophytos, and sancti-

8. *Saint Neophytos in prayer, between the Archangels Michael and Gabriel. Wallpainting of the bema of the Engleistra. 1183.*

fy, O merciful, the souls of them that sleep not in the night". The Virgin and John the Baptist are depicted praying in two small medallions which touch the medallion in which Christ Pantocrator is painted. These wall paintings which constitute the Supplication, were made in 1503.

On the wall that separates the bema from the Saint's cell the Annunciation of the Virgin is painted. In this scene Christ–Immanuel is depicted standing between Archangel Gabriel and the Virgin in a separate frame.

On the west side of the holy bema and on the west part of the north side seven Saints Ascetics are painted: Efraim the Syrian, Kyriakos the Anchorite, Theodoros the Sanctified, Pahomios, Ilarion and Efthymios.

4. The wall paintings of the Saint's cell

In the west part of the cell there is the stone bed of the Saint 0,40m high, 0,63m wide and 1,73m long. Behind the bed there is a rectangular niche in which the books of the Saint were kept. In front of the bed there is a built table covered with a flat slab 0,85×0,56m which was used by the Saint as desk. In the northeast end of the cell the Saint's tomb is hewn in the rock. On the east wall of the cell there is a narrow and low entrance which, according to some tradition, was opened following the discovery of the relics of the Saint in 1756 to allow women to visit the Saint's tomb. Two small windows high on the east wall allow light to get through into the Saint's cell.

The ceiling of the cell is completely uneven. At its top Prophets are painted in medallions. Only one has survived in good condition, Daniel. Of Isaiah only the name has survived. Of the third prophet the head and the name have been destroyed. But the body and the roll on which verse 9 of the 46th Psalm is written have survived. This does not necessarily mean that he is David. He may be one of the major Prophets, Ezekiel or Jeremiah. It is not certain that there was a fourth medallion also. Between the Prophets and the east wall the half destroyed head of a Saint, whose name, Saint Damianos, survived until 60 years ago, has survived. There is also a very badly damaged inscription which refers to the relation of Saint Neophytos with the Monastery of Agios Chrysostomos Koutsovendi.

The east wall of the cell was decorated with five, most probably, standing military Saints. Today only three have survived, very badly damaged though, and traces of a fourth are visible. There survives the name of only one, the first from the left, but half destroyed. {Theodo}ros Stratelatis. The others have been identified with Saint Demetrios and Saint Prokopios.

On the south wall of the cell there are two layers of paintings. Only small parts of the oldest are discernible. It seems that originally the Crucifixion scene was somewhat more narrow and in it apart from Crucified Christ only the Virgin and Saint John the Evangelist were depicted, while more to the east another Saint in a broader frame is depicted. Today at the east end of the south wall there survives the lower half of a man in royal clothes completely unidentified. There follows the scene of Crucifixion. Christ is half destroyed. To the right of Christ only remnants from the Virgin and the two Myrrhbearers accompanying her have survived. John the Evangelist and the centurion have survived in a better condition. At the west end of the south wall there survives the upper part of Saint Andrew, the fool for Christ, who is depicted standing.

It seems that to the east of the narrow door that joins the cell with the bema two Saints, most probably military, were depicted standing. Today only some traces have survived. The jambs of the narrow door were also decorated with standing Saints, as the traces on the west jamb of the door indicate.

In the west side of the cell, where the stone bed and the library of the Saint are, there were no painted human figures. Only an imitation of a marble revetment covers the space over the bed and the Saint's library.

The west half of the north wall is decorated with the Supplication.

9. Supplication. Wallpainting in the cell of Saint Neophytos. 1183.

29

In the middle Christ is seated on a backless throne. He is blessing with His right hand raised in front of the chest and with the left holding a closed book. To the right of Christ the Virgin is depicted standing and turned to the left with the hands extended in front in prayer while to the left of Christ St. John the Baptist is depicted praying. Below, on the left, Saint Neophytos is depicted kneeling turned to the left. With his two hands he is holding the right foot of Christ. In front of him there is an open roll on which his prayer is inscribed: "By the prayers of Thy Mother and Thy Baptist who stand reverently by Thy holy throne, be Thou merciful, O Christ, now and evermore to him that lies a supplicant at Thy divine foot". There are extensive changes in the painting of the Supplication, which, however, are due to the painter who re-painted it and to his effort to render the scene better.

Beneath the Supplication there is a half-destroyed inscription which mentions the name of the painter: "The Engleistra... was painted completely by the hand of Theodoros Apseudes in the year 6691 indiction 1". The year 6691 from the creation of the world corresponds to the year 1183. As is known the Byzantines believed that Christ was born in the year 5508 from the creation of the world. Thus deducting the year 5508 from the year 6691 we find the year 1183. This year is confirmed also by Saint Neophytos himself in his Ritual Ordinance.

On the east half of the north wall there is the niche in which Saint Neophytos himself hewed his tomb. Between the wall painting of the Supplication and his grave there is a badly damaged medical Saint and a half-destroyed inscription which refers to the tomb of Saint Neophytos.

The niche in which the tomb of the Saint is, is decorated on its three sides. On the west side the Crucifixion of Christ, which has been badly damaged, is painted. At the west end of the north side a shallow niche has been hewn in which the Virgin is painted enthroned with Christ. She is holding Christ with the left hand while with the right she is holding a roll with the following inscription: "Grant O my Son, remission to him that lies here+I grant it, moved as I am by thy prayers".

On either side of the Virgin Saint John Chrysostom, who is turned to the Crucifixion, and Saint Basil, who is turned to the scene of the Resurrection of Christ, are painted. The scene of the Resurrection of Christ is painted in the greater part of the north side and on the east side of the niche in which the Saint's tomb is. As is customary in Byzantine Art the Resurrection of Christ is depicted with His Descent to Hell. Christ after His Crucifixion descended to Hell and smashed the gates of Hell and preached to the dead lying there for centuries who believed in him. Christ in this scene is depicted standing over the smashed Gates of the Hell and pulling Adam with his left hand in order to resurrect him. Eve is depicted behind Adam. To the left of Christ, David, Solomon and John the Baptist are painted in the same sarcophagus, together with Adam and Eve, to represent the human race.

10. The Resurrection (Descent into Hell), wallpainting in the tomb of Saint Neophytos. 1183.

5. The Refectory of the Monastery of the Engleistra

The Refectory of the Monastery of the Engleistra or the "Refectory tou Aristou" (*ariston* means the lunch), as Saint Neophytos calls it, is to the north of the Saint's cell. Like all Byzantine Refectories this too was originally completely decorated with wall paintings. Today only a small part of these wall paintings has survived.

On the south wall the Virgin is depicted enthroned between Archangels holding the Christ Child. Unfortunately the heads of all have been destroyed. But a large part of this wall painting has survived and this helps us date it to the end of the 12th century. On the east wall and the west wall ascetics were depicted standing in a frontal position holding rolls as in the west wall of the church of the Engleistra. Today three have survived on the east wall and nine on the west in very bad condition. On the west wall, over the standing Saintly monks there are two layers of wall paintings. On the more recent layer, the one the visitor sees, martyrdoms of Saints seem to have been depicted. On the southeast part of the ceiling parts of three medallions, which contained the upper parts of prophets, have survived. Only the name of one of them has survived: Elias. From the inscription that accompanied the third medallion only the word Proph(et) has survived. The medallions are painted in a yellowish background which is decorated with very stylised ivy and vine leaves.

THE MAIN CHURCH OF THE MONASTERY
OF AGIOS NEOPHYTOS

The Catholikon, that is the main church, of the Monastery, was built most probably early in the 16th century as its architectural style indicates. It is a basilica with a dome and the influence of Venetian architecture is evident. The aisles of the church are separated by 2 colonnades which consist of four columns each. After the demolition of the original west wall of the church and the incorporation of the narthex in the church the engaged piers of the west wall became rectangular pillars which prop up not only the west semicircular arch of each colonnade but also the broad pointed arch in the extension of the colonnade of the church which divided the narthex into three aisles. It is not known when the narthex was incorporated in the church. But it seems that this was done before 1735 because Barsky, who visited the Monastery at the time, says the church had no narthex. The columns of the two colonnades of the church have pseudocorinthian capitals which are characteristic of the Venetian Renaissance. The zone with the thornleaves at the base of the dome and the shape of the windows of the church are also due to Venetian influence.

The whole of the Main Church was decorated with wall paintings of which only a small part has survived. Its dedication to the Virgin dictated the iconographic programme. On the dome and in the west vault of the middle aisle no wall paintings have survived. On the east vault of the middle aisle over the bema preliminary carbon drawings were found of the Ascension of Christ and the Pentecost, two scenes which from the Middle Byzantine period were painted in this location.

The cycle of the life of Christ was very probably painted on the west vault of the middle aisle and on the west wall.

The vault of the south aisle, as indicated by the traces which have survived until today, was decorated with the cycle of the life of the Virgin, a widespread practice in that period. Indeed at the east end of the south half of the south vault the first two scenes of the cycle of the life of the Virgin, the Offer and the Rejection of the gifts of Joachim and Anna because they were childless, are depicted followed by the Prayer of Joachim. If we are to judge by the icons of the Enriched Dodecaorton, which are contemporary with the wall paintings and most probably the work of the same painter, the scenes of the Prayer of Anna, the Embracing of Joachim and Anna, the Birth of the Virgin, the Caressing of the Virgin, the Presentation of the Virgin into the Temple, the Betrothal of the Virgin and others we find on the west vault and on the west wall of the church of the True Cross at Pelendri must have followed. The vault of the north aisle is decorated with the 24 stanzas of the Akathistos. The stanza "She showed a new world" was painted on the spandrel which closed the north vault in the west.

The Akathistos, which is a hymn to the Virgin, consists of 24 stanzas and is chanted during Lent, that is the period of fasting before Easter. On the evening of each Friday of the first four weeks six stanzas are chanted and on the evening of the Friday of the fifth week of the period of fasting the entire Akathistos is chanted. Every stanza starts with a letter of the Greek Alphabet. The Hymn starts from the east end of the south half of the vault and continues as far as the west end. Thus Stanzas A–M are painted. Stanza N was painted on the west wall which was demolished. There follow the rest of the Stanzas Ξ–Ω from the west end of the north half of the vault and continue until the east end. At the top of the east wall of the north aisle of the church which closes the north vault the Trinity is painted according to the western iconography.

11. The Prayer of Joachim. Wallpainting of the vault of the south aisle of the main Church of the Monastery of Agios Neophytos. Around 1544.

12. "The shepherds heard", Stanza H΄ of the Akathistos intext Hymn. Wallpainting of the vault of the north, aisle of the main church of the Monastery of Agios Neophytos. Around 1544.

13. *"Having seen the running star the Magi" and "The Children of the Chaldaeans saw" Stanzas Θ and I of the Acathist Hymn. Wallpainting of the vault of the north aisle of the Church of the Monastery of Agios Neophytos around 1544.*

The wall paintings of the apse

According to the customary practice, the Virgin is painted in the semidome of the apse, enthroned with Christ on her lap between Archangels Michael and Gabriel. A large part of this wall painting has been destroyed. Below on the semicircular wall of the apse the Giving of the Bread is painted to the north of the window and to the south of

14. "Willing to save the world". Stanza Σ of the Acathist Hymn. Wallpainting of the vault of the north aisle of the Church of the Monastery of Agios Neophytos. Around 1544.

the window the Giving of the Wine. In the first scene Christ, under a canopy and in front of a table on which the Paten is placed, gives the Apostles the Bread. Peter is the first to extend the hands and receive the Bread from Christ. There follow another five Apostles. The head of the last Apostle, on the left has been destroyed. Above this scene it is written from right to left "Take it. This is my body which is given for you. This do in remembrance of me". The fact that the writing is from right to left is not due to an influence of semitic writing but to the desire of the painter, or the person who instructed that the scene be painted, that the phrase start from Christ who uttered these words. In the Giving of the Wine scene Christ is depicted again beneath a canopy and in front of the table, turned to the left holding a Chalice with which he offers

+ ΤΟΥΤΟΝ ΤΟΝΟΙΚΟΝ ΟΓΗΡ ΟΚΟΔΟΜΗCΕΝ ΤΟΥ ΤΟΝ ΤΟΝ ΟΙΚΟΝ ΟΥΟC ΕΤΕΡΑΙΩCΕΝ· ΤΟΥΤΟΝ ΤΟΝ ΟΙΚΟΝ. ΤΟΓΠΑ ΤΟΔΓΠΟΝ ΑΝΕΚΕΝΙCΕΝ·

15. "Take it". Wallpainting in the apse of the Church of the Monastery of Agios Neophytos. Around 1544.

the Wine to Apostle Paul who is at the head of the other five Apostles. Above the head of Christ there starts the phrase "Drink it all of it for this is my blood of the New Testament which is shed for many for the remission of sins". In both scenes an Angel deacon holds an exaptery-gon. On the sides of the large window of the apse at the level of the "Communion" of the Apostles two Angels are depicted turned to the two scenes of the "Communion". Both wear habits of deacons. The Angel who is turned to the "Giving of the Bread" scene is holding in both hands a lit candle, while the Angel who is turned to the "Offering of the Wine" scene holds with the right hand a censer and is censing and with the left a lit candle.

In the lower part of the semicylindrical wall of the apse six prelates

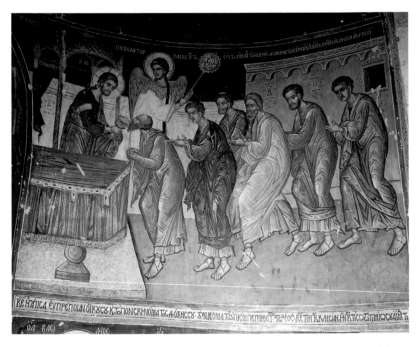

16. "Drink it all". Wallpainting in the apse of the Church of the Monastery of Agios Neophytos. Around 1544.

are depicted officiating. The Prelates are in two groups. Each group consists of three Prelates turned to the centre of the apse where the Altar is depicted beneath the window. On the left Saints Athanasios, Gregory the Theologian and John Chrysostom are depicted dresed in bishop's vestments and turned to the left. In their hands they hold rolls on which prayers recited at Mass are written. On the right Saints Basil, Cyril of Alexandria and John the Almoner are depicted wearing bishop's vestments. They too hold rolls on which prayers read by the priest during Mass are written. Above the prelates there are the following inscriptions. Left: "O Lord this house the Father built, this house the Son made sound. This house the Spirit renovated". On the right: "O Lord I loved the beauty of your house and the place of your glory. Being the

17. Saints John Chrysostom, Gregory the Theologian and Athanasios officiating. Wallpainting, in the apse of the Church of the Monastery of Agios Neophytos. Around 1544.

support of these who have believed in You. O Lord make sound the church you built with Your holy blood".

On the east wall, north of the apse a flying Angel is depicted in a starry sky covering the face with his habit and at a lower level the "Descent from the Cross", i.e. Christ–Utter Humiliation, badly damaged. In the nearby semicircular niche St. Stephen, the first martyr, is painted. South of the apse on the east wall deacon Saint Lavrentios is painted, to the right of it St. Sylvester, pope of Rome, is depicted. In the semicircular niche beneath the wall painting of St. Silvester an Angel

41

18. Saints Basil, Cyril of Alexandria and John the Almoner officiating. Wallpainting in the apse of the Church of Agios Neophytos Monastery.

deacon is depicted holding the dead Christ (= Meslismos) on a purple cloth. To the right of the niche a candle is painted and above it there is an inscription which refers to Christ–Melismos: "Here I lie a lamb secretly sacrificed; I'm dismembered and feed the Pious. Take care, Man, not to eat unworthily".

19. Angel holding the shroud with Christ (Amnos–melismos).
Wallpainting in a niche of the east wall of the Church of the
Monastery of Agios Neophytos. Around 1544.

The other wall paintings of the church

Beneath the cycle of the life of the Virgin in the south aisle some traces of the wall painting of the Council of 843 at Constantinople which decided the restoration of the icons survived. The Councils were most probably depicted on the south wall.

In the soffit of the first arch, from the east, of the south colonnade two standing Prelates are depicted, Saint Ignatios and Saint Timotheos. In the soffit of the second arch of the same colonnade Saints Alexios, the man of God, and Saint John Kalyvitis (living in a hut) are depicted. In the soffit of the third arch of the south colonnade Saint Hilarion is depicted. The head of Saint Hilarion has been destroyed. The wall painting which was in the west half of this soffit has been destroyed. Above the first column, from the east, of the south colonnade Saint Damianos is depicted on the south side and above the second column of the same colonnade Saint Kosmas. On the east side of the west engaged pier of the south colonnade Saint Paraskevi is depicted.

High on the east wall of the north aisle the Trinity is depicted, in western iconography: in an arch of heavens. God the Father, Christ and the Holy Spirit in the form of a Pigeon, instead of the usual representation of the Hospitality of Abraham in Byzantine art. God Father and Christ are depicted in busts, blessing with the right hand and with the left God Father holding a roll and Christ a closed book. Outside the arch of heavens three exapteryga are depicted and below, on the left, Just [Laz]ar[os]. On the north wall Saints Eleftherios and Ypatios in bishop's vestments are depicted beneath the Stanza Ψ "Chanting your birthgiving" of the again avaration in spelling Acathist Hymn. Above the third column, from the east, of the north colonnade Saint Samonas is painted. Finally in the east half of the soffit of the fourth arch from the east Saint Elpidiforos is depicted, half destroyed.

The iconostasis

The central and the south part of the iconostasis are the original. The north part of the iconostasis was destroyed and replaced recently by another, which is a copy of the south part. The original iconostasis was made in the 16th century and is contemporary with the church. It is one of the very few examples of 16th century woodcarving which has survived in Cyprus.

On the iconostasis there are 16th century icons of outstanding art and more specifically of 1544. These are the icons of the Great Supplication in the highest row of the iconostasis and the icons of the Dodecaorton. The Cross and the Lypira (that is the Virgin, Saint John the Evangelist) the Utter Humiliation, Risen Christ which are at the top of the iconostasis, belong to the same period. The large icons with the exception of those of Christ, the Virgin and John the Baptist, are more recent, of the 19th century. Some of them, like Saint Anthony, Saint John the Evangelist, Saint Nicholas and Saints Peter and Paul, were repainted in 1951. The icon of Saint Neophytos is a work of Ioannis Kornaros and was painted in 1806. The icons of Christ and the Virgin are 16th century works while that of Saint John the Baptist was made a little later.

Originally the icons of the enriched Dodecaorton were 26. Of the original icons only 22 have survived, some of them badly damaged. On these icons scenes from the life of the Virgin and Christ are depicted. 1) Joachim and Anna offering gifts and the return of the gifts. 2) Joachim praying in the mountain. 3) Anna praying in her garden and the Embracing of Joachim and Anna. 4) The Birth of the Virgin. 5) The Caressing of the Virgin. 6) The Presentation of the Virgin into the Temple. 7) The Birth of Christ. 8) The Transfiguration of Christ. 9) The Raising of Lazarus. 10) The Entry into Jerusalem. 11) The Last Supper. 12) The Washing of the Feet, 13) The Betrayal. 14) Jesus before High Priests Annas and Caiphas. 15) The way to Calvary,. 16) The Crucifixion. 17) The Descent from the Cross. 18) The Lamentation.

20. The central part of the iconostasis of the Church.

19) The Resurrection. 20) The Ascension. 21) The Pentecost. 22) The Dormition of the Virgin.

The Great Supplication icons were originally 17. Today only 16 have survived. In the centre of the row the upper part of Christ in a frontal position is depicted. To the right of Christ there are 2) The Virgin 3) Saint Peter and 4) Archangel Michael. To the left of Christ the following are depicted 5) Saint John the Baptist, 6) Saint Paul, 7) Archangel Gabriel. There follow in the part of the iconostasis which is in the north aisle Saints 8) Thomas 9) Matthew 10) Bartholomew 11) Luke and in the part of the iconostasis which is in the south aisle Saints 12) John the Evangelist 13) Philip 14) James 15) Mark and 16) Andrew.

According to the inscriptions which are at the back of the icon of Christ and of Saints Peter and Paul and of the two Archangels the icons are works of Iosif Khouris and were painted in 1544.

The icons of the Dodekaorton are not dated and not signed by the painter who painted them. The technique and style of these icons, however, are similar to the technique and style of the icons of the Great Supplication painted by Iosif Khouris in 1544.

The woodcarved Pulpit with the icons of the Evangelists was made in 1883 at the time Gregorios was Abbot. At the time of Abbot Gregorios the abbot's throne was also made in 1858. The silver reliquary which contains the skull of Saint Neophytos was made in 1802 and is a donation of Archimandrite Ioannikios of the Archbishopric of Cyprus.

21. The Nativity, icon, 52×41 cm. Church of the Monastery of Agios Neophytos. 1544.

22. The Transfiguration, icon, 52,5×42,5 cm. Church of the Monastery of Agios Neophytos. 1544.

49

23. The Entry into Jerusalem, icon, 51,5×41 cm. Church of the Monastery of Agios Neophytos. 1544.

24. *The Crucifixion, icon, 52,5×42,5 cm. Church of the Monastery of Agios Neophytos. 1544.*

25. The Archangel St. Michael, icon, 83×69,5 cm. Church of the Monastery of Agios Neophytos. 1544.

*26. Saint John the Apostle, icon, 56,5×48 cm. Church of the Monastery of Agios
Neophytos. 1544.*

THE MUSEUM OF THE MONASTERY

The Monastery in order to protect its treasures and also to make them available to visitors has created, under the east wing of the Monastery, a Museum in which significant treasures are on display. The Museum consists of two sections, the purely ecclesiastical in which icons, sacred vessels and clerical vestments from the 12th until the 19th century are exhibited and the non-ecclesiastical in which pottery of the Geometric and Archaic Periods in Cyprus (roughly 900–600 BC) are on display.

The visitor goes down to the Museum by a staircase in the north end of the east wing, west of the portico and enters the anteroom where the custodian's office is. Here there are icons of small dimensions mainly of the 19th century. Only one icon, that of the Enthroned Virgin holding Christ in her lap, is of large dimensions. This icon was made as recently as 1884.

The anteroom is separated from the Ist room by a big showcase containing a wooden antimension (portable altar) of 1684, two Chalices and two Patens of the 19th century, three 19th century carved wooden crosses, the one half-destroyed, with a silver base and a silver frame, a small wooden box decorated with coloured inlay and of mother of pearl inlay, a many-coloured carved wooden sarcophagus shaped reliquary, two Chalices with embroidered cross shaped chalice covers of the 19th century, 18th and 19th century silver buckles and mother of pearl buckles of various shapes and styles and a Russian Artoforion (pyx).

In the first room of the Museum some very important icons are on display. 1) Jesus Christ the Philanthropos, probably work of painter

27. Jesus Christ the Philanthropos. 73×46 cm. Museum of the Monastery of Agios Neophytos. 1183.

Theodoros Apseudes, who painted the wall paintings of the cell and the bema of the Engleistra in 1183. The head of Christ seems to have been destroyed and painted again early in the 16th century. 2) Virgin Eleousa, work of painter Theodoros Apseudes as indicated by the style. The Virgin's upper part has been painted, turned to the left with the hands extended as if in supplication. These two icons date back to the last quarter of the 12th century.

28. *The Virgin Eleousa, 73×46 cm. Museum of the Monastery of Agios Neophytos. 1183.*

The other icons were made later. Noteworthy are two icons in a woodcarved frame. They depict Archangels Michael and Gabriel and originally were most probably at the top of the iconostasis of the main church of the Monastery. The painting style is the same as that of the Great Supplication icons on the iconostasis and, consequently, contemporary. They are most probably works of painter Iosif Khouris who painted also the Great Supplication icons in 1544. The royal doors

29. Archangel Gabriel 83×40 cm. Museum of the Monastery of Agios Neophytos. 16th century.

(dimensions 150×94,5 cm) which originally belonged to the iconostasis were made during the same period. On the upper part of these royal doors the Annunciation of the Virgin and below, on the left side, Saint Gregory the Theologian and Saint John Chrysostom and on the right Saint Basil and Saint Neophytos are painted.

Older is the icon of Saint Neophytos (dimensions 126, 5×62,6 cm) donation of monk Neophytos who is described as the new founder of the Monastery and who died in 1512. Another icon that may be dated to the second half of the 16th century or early in the 17th century is that of the three prelates Saint Basil, John Chrysostom and Gregory the Theologian.

In the second room there are on display royal doors which date to the end of the 18th century. They are in a relatively good condition. Depicted on them are, above, the Annunciation of the Virgin, and, below, on the left Saint Basil and John Chrysostom and, on the right, Saints Gregory the Theologian and Saint Nicholas.

Other icons exhibited in the second room are that of Saint John the Baptist, painted in 1794, as the relevant inscription on the back of the icon says, that of Saint Antonios, which dates to 1819, that of Saint Gregory in 1845, the icons of Saints Vycheanos, and the 40 Holy Martyrs of Sebasteia, of Saint Hermogenes and of the Entry into Jerusalem, which date to the 19th century.

The Cross with Crucified Christ and Lypiron, in which the Virgin is depicted, date to the end of the 16th century. Both the Cross and the lypiron come from the church of Agios Kendeas in the town of Paphos.

On display in this room are four censers, the oldest dating to 1691 and the most recent to early 20th century.

On display in the same room are various gospels with silver gilded covers. 1) On the cover of the first gospel there is in front a silver gilded plate in relief decoration. In the middle the Crucifixion of Christ surrounded by scenes from the Passion. At the back on the cover the Resurrection of Christ is depicted, and around the appearances of

*30. Saint Neophytos. 126,5×62,5. Museum of
the Monastery of Agios Neophytos. Around 1500.*

Christ to His disciples after his Resurrection. Below the Resurrection
of Christ an inscription mentions the donor, Abbot Chrysanthos,
physician, and the date 1848. 2) On the leather cover of the second
Gospel there is a silver gilded cross depicting the Resurrection of

Christ and at the edges of the arms of the Cross, above the Preparation, on the left John the Evangelist, on the right the Virgin and below Saint Neophytos on his knees, praying. In the corners the 4 Evangelists are depicted on silver plates. 3) On the cover of the third gospel in front, in silver plates the Resurrection of Christ in the middle and the four Evangelists are depicted with their symbols in the corners. On the back, the upper part of Saint Neophytos is depicted in relief on a silver medallion.

In this room manuscripts and old printed books are also on display in showcases. The oldest manuscript, with the beginning and the end missing, contains sermons of Saint Neophytos on the gospel and dates to the end of the 12th century or early in the 13th century. Another paper codex, handwritten, also with the beginning and the end missing, may be dated to the 16th–17th century. It is a lectionary. A short prayer book which contains the Mass written by John Chrysostom and Saint Basil and the ordination ceremony for Anagnostis, sub deacon, deacon and priest was written by monk Ioannikios Kykkotis in 1698.

The other manuscripts are largely musical and date to the 18h and 19th centuries.

The oldest manuscript on display in the Museum is a piece of papyrus, dimensions 15×13 cm, and dates to the 6th century.

There are also books containing writings of Saint Neophytos edited in Venice in 1779. In a show–case on the east wall in the second room there are on display gold embroidered maniples (cuffs) and "epigonatia" (= an embroidered rectangular piece of cloth attached to the waist above the tunic, through a cord and reaching down to the knee). On the first pair of maniples, which date to the 17th or 18th century, the Annunciation of the Virgin is embroidered. On the second pair of the maniples, which date to the 19th century, there are embroidered crosses. On one of the "epigonatia" the Last Supper and on the second Christ seated on a backless throne are embroidered. On the third "epigonation", which is more recent, there are an embroidered cross and decorations.

In the third room there are on display icons, minor objects and a stole.

The most significant icon, even though it has been repainted, is Panagia Engleistriani, donation of the former abbot Ioakeim and work of painter Theophylaktos, an early 16th century painter. The former abbot Ioakeim is depicted kneeling and praying to the Virgin.

Another icon is the "Descent from the Cross (=Epitaph–Lamentation). Here Christ is depicted lying in a shroud. It may be dated to the 17th century.

A Russian triptych is significant. In the centre of the triptych the Coronation of the Virgin, a subject alien to the Orthodox Tradition, is painted. On the right leaf Archangel Michael and Jesus of Nevi, above, and Saint John of Bronz and Saint Nicholas, below, are depicted. On the left leaf Archangel Gabriel and Prophet Daniel are depicted, above, and Saint Demetrios Bishop of Rostovsk, and Saint George, below. Next to it on display is also the silver revetment of the triptych. The icon of Saint Neophytos is dated to 1888.

The minor objects in a show–case on the left include pectoral crosses, bracelets, reliquaries and buckles and the seal of the bishop of Paphos Epiphanios (1890–1899).

In a show–case between the 3rd and the 4th room there are on display a gilded Chalice of 1848 and a silver Paten of 1848, both donated by economos Chrysanthos, physician, a 19th century silver candlestick, a bronze 18th–19th century oenochoe, a receptacle of holy water, and two rose water receptacles, the one made of glass, of the 19th century, and the other made of silver, of 1911. There are also on display 3 handles of an abbot's staff. The one has an inscription and the date 1864.

In the fourth room of the Museum there are a 17th–18th century icon of Saint Neophytos, four pieces from royal doors fixed on the south wall, which date to the 16th century. Depicted on these pieces are standing Prelates, the large icon of the Dormition of the Virgin donation of Neophytos the monk, who died in 1511, a small icon of Panagia tou Kykkou of 1815 and also abbot's staffs of the 18th–19th century and candles, wooden with painted decoration or with silver revetment, of the 19th and early 20th century.

The visitor coming out of this room enters the large room on the west where the Geometric and Archaic Period (roughly 900–600 BC) pottery are on display and leaves by the staircase built into the north end of the Museum.

BIBLIOGRAPHY

F. E. WARREN. The Ritual Ordinance of St. Neophytos.

I. ΧΑΤΖΗΙΩΑΝΝΟΥ. Ιστορία και έργα του Αγίου Νεοφύτου του Εγκλείστου. Αλεξάνδρεια 1914.

Α.Κ. ΙΝΔΙΑΝΟΥ και G. TOMSON. "Wall paintings at St. Neophytos Monastery". (Κυπριακές Σπουδές 1939, σελ. 155-224).

I. ΤΣΙΚΝΟΠΟΥΛΟΥ. Η Ιερά Μονή του Αγίου Νεοφύτου. Πάφος 1955.

Γ. ΣΩΤΗΡΙΟΥ. Τα Βυζαντινά Μνημεία της Κύπρου. Αθήναι 1935.

C. MANGO and E.J.W. HAWKINS. The Hermitage of St. Neophytos and its Wall Paintings. D.O.P. XX 1966 p. 136-206.

A. and J. STYLIANOU. The Painted Churches of Cyprus. London 1985.

CONTENTS